Original title:
Finding Meaning in the Mess

Copyright © 2025 Creative Arts Management OÜ
All rights reserved.

Author: Olivia Sterling
ISBN HARDBACK: 978-1-80566-160-3
ISBN PAPERBACK: 978-1-80566-455-0

Unveiling the Untangled

In the kitchen, eggs cracked wide,
Flour storms swirl, a bumpy ride.
I laugh as I slip on a gooey floor,
This messy life, who could ask for more?

Socks mismatched, where's my left shoe?
My morning coffee tastes slightly askew.
Yet in this chaos, joy often peeks,
With giggles and grins, it's fun that speaks.

Threads of Hope woven in Fear

Stitching together dreams with thread,
While tangled yarn has my hopes misled.
But who needs a pattern, a perfect design?
My quilt of quirks turns out just fine!

The cat pounces, aiming for my yarn,
Causing mayhem, a fashionably torn.
Yet laughter erupts as I rescue my spool,
In this wild dance, I feel like a fool.

Chaos as a Catalyst

Juggling dishes, a pyramid of cups,
Here comes the cat, with wild little hops.
Down goes the tower, clatter, and crash,
Yet somehow, we giggle as we make a splash.

Paint splatters decorate the walls,
A masterpiece made of careless calls.
Creativity blooms in the mess we've made,
In chaos, my laughter is never delayed.

Finding Footsteps in Fragments

Pieces of puzzles lie in disarray,
I trip on the corners while searching away.
Yet each clumsy step, a dance in disguise,
In this broken ballet, hilarity flies.

My garden's a jungle, weeds in a swirl,
But amidst all the chaos, flowers unfurl.
With muddy knees, I witness their grace,
In every odd turn, I find my own place.

The Hidden Gems of Life's Puzzles

In a jumble of socks where the lost ones play,
A partner in crime went astray.
With mismatched shoes on this fashion spree,
I trip on my dreams, but oh, do I see!

The cat steals my lunch, what a cheeky brat,
She thinks she's the queen, and I'm just the mat.
Each day is a quest for the brightest delight,
In this riddle of chaos, I'm shining bright!

Embracing the Torn Edges

A shirt with a hole is a badge of pride,
It tells wild tales of adventures wide.
Stains may be there, but they're part of the fun,
Each messy moment is a victory won!

The crusty toast feels like art on the plate,
Every burn and char add to my fate.
With laughter, I savor, my kitchen a wreck,
Like Picasso's brush, I just might collect!

Threads of Hope in Tattered Fabric

A quilt full of patches, some pink, some blue,
Stitched up with laughter and a few strands of glue.
Each tiny snag carries a story untold,
Of cozy warmth in the chaos so bold!

The blanket of life is frayed at the seams,
But soft are the dreams in the midst of the screams.
I wrap up in joy, like a burrito, I chill,
In tangled threads, I find laughter's thrill!

The Dance of Muddled Footsteps

A two-step on marbles, a wiggle and slip,
In this dance of my life, I'm taking a trip.
Though rhythm may stumble, I'll twirl and I'll sway,
With laughter my partner, come what may!

The music's a mix of the good and the bad,
It's strange, it's chaotic, but makes me so glad.
With each wobbly move, I embrace all the zest,
In this tangle of life, I'm loving the mess!

Tangled Threads of Purpose

In a basket, all things tangle,
Socks and spoons, a messy jangle.
Life's a puzzle, quirky and odd,
But from this chaos, magic's trod.

Lost my keys, they're under a shoe,
Coffee spills, what's old becomes new.
Dishes pile up, a mountain of fate,
Yet laughter's the spice we appreciate.

Juggling dreams like oranges tossed,
With every drop, never feel lost.
Giggles hide in the jumbled space,
A dance of folly, life's wild grace.

So here we are, in cluttered delight,
Searching for gold in the ridiculous sight.
Tangled threads weave stories bold,
In this crazy mess, life unfolds.

The Beauty in Broken Pieces

A vase once grand now lies in shards,
Each piece tells tales, life's funny cards.
A cereal bowl with a smiley crack,
In this buffet of chaos, we never lack.

Toed the line on a Lego floor,
A masterpiece of pain, oh, what a score!
Dances interrupted by a pet's wild chase,
Messy moments hold the silliest grace.

Pieces broken but hearts still mend,
With every hiccup, we learn to blend.
Sprinkles on chaos, a cupcake parade,
Laughter's the frosting, let joy cascade.

So gather the fragments, don't be shy,
Find beauty where the odd things lie.
In the mess of life, with humor we seize,
Life's a jigsaw, a puzzle with ease.

Luminous Whispers from Chaos

In the kitchen, it's utter mayhem,
Spaghetti flung like a noodle gem.
Dancing crumbs embark on a spree,
Whispers of laughter, wild jubilee.

Laundry's a rainbow, clothes on the floor,
Each hue a laugh, nothing's a bore.
Socks mate under the couch's deep shade,
In this wacky world, no need to evade.

Coffee stains etch a morning story,
Baked goods flop but it's not so hoary.
Spills and thrills, oh what a delight,
In twisted moments, the heart takes flight.

So let's embrace the chaos unfurled,
In each blunder, a miracle swirled.
Luminous whispers guide us along,
In the carnival mess, where we belong.

In the Midst of Disarray

Upon the desk, papers skedaddle,
A renegade pen leads a wild battle.
Sticky notes blossom, like flowers absurd,
In disarray, brilliance is stirred.

Forgotten sandwich under the bed,
Leggo of worries, let giggles spread.
Tangled up cords, a technology mess,
Each knot a riddle, surely to bless.

Through the clutter, shines a bright cake,
Uneven frosting, but it's ours to make.
Life's little blunders, a grand symphony,
In the erratic, we find camaraderie.

So let's toast to this topsy-turvy ride,
In disorder's arms, we take proud stride.
Joy's in the hiccups, the laughs that we play,
In the midst of disarray, come what may.

A Palette of Hues in Dissonance

In a world of mismatched socks,
The rainbow shouts, 'I'm lost!'
Colors clash, a reminder loud,
Chaos wears a vibrant coat.

Jumbled thoughts in a blender spin,
Like a cat that plays with yarn.
We twirl and laugh in disarray,
Finding joy in every turn.

The Beauty Beneath the Scar

A coffee stain upon the rug,
A tapestry of morning blight.
Yet laughter hides beneath the spill,
Each fault, a tickle in the fight.

Pillow forts and sticky notes,
Life's confetti tossed around.
Diving deep in every flaw,
The beauty there, so tightly wound.

Journeys Through the Jumble

Maps are scribbles, roads askew,
I tripped on every twist and turn.
Yet in the stumble, I found grace,
Lessons learned, my heart's bright burn.

Lost my keys beneath the couch,
A treasure hunt in chaos reigns.
Through the mess, my spirit soars,
Each mishap, joy like autumn rains.

Reflection in the Ruckus

Mirrors cracked and voices loud,
Reflections dance in kooky styles.
Each echo carries tales so wild,
We laugh at life's absurd profiles.

The kitchen's a circus, pots collide,
As I cook with flair and zest.
In every crash, a clinking tune,
Ruckus sings, we're truly blessed.

Whirlwind Wisdom

In a world where socks collide,
And the toaster's gone awry,
The cat sits on the keyboard,
As I just wonder why.

Coffee spills on yesterday,
As the dog digs through the trash,
Life's a wild rollercoaster,
With a twist and a great crash.

But in the chaos of our days,
There's laughter, bright and loud,
A dance of mismatched moments,
We're a beautiful, silly crowd.

So I'll embrace this crazy ride,
With a giggle and a cheer,
For within this wacky whirlwind,
I'll find joy year after year.

Echoes from the Abyss

In the depths where socks are lost,
Lives a legend or a ghost,
The dishes stack like ancient ruins,
A symphony of what we boast.

Fridge magnets hold our secrets tight,
While leftovers waltz with glee,
A tale of chaos we recite,
In the land of laundry spree.

Yet amidst the scattered chaos,
Are echoes of our quirks,
Like dancing shadows in the night,
Or comic cuts and smirks.

So I'll raise a toast to the absurd,
To the messes that we weave,
For in this loud cacophony,
There's magic we believe.

Roots of Resilience

In the garden of forgotten toys,
Dandelions bloom with grace,
Life tips its hat in funny ways,
As giggles fill the space.

Potatoes grow where we once fought,
With weeds that tell us tales,
Of chaos sprouting in full bloom,
As laughter never fails.

The scattered seeds of whimsy,
Root deep in messy soil,
Through tangled vines and silly paths,
We find joy in our toil.

So I'll dance with dirt-stained shoes,
In this quirky, wild quest,
For in every twisted venture,
We find moments we love best.

Letters to the Lost

Dear mismatched sock, where'd you roam?
I searched high, I searched low,
Your partner's now a loner,
With nowhere left to go.

To the spoon that plays hide and seek,
You're a master of disguise,
With forks that wobble, laugh and squeak,
As the pizza slice just flies.

And to the dust bunnies so spry,
You dance in corners so bold,
Your antics make me laugh out loud,
Like tales that never get old.

So here's a toast to all that's lost,
In this quirky, bustling din,
For in each tear and goofy grin,
We find the joy within.

Chaos's Gentle Embrace

In the kitchen, flour flies,
A cake mix turned into a pie.
Eggs dance on the floor like wild birds,
Who knew baking could end in such absurd words?

Tangled wires that should connect,
My headphones now a fine architect.
I untie them with a laugh so loud,
Messy joys should always be proud!

Sock puppets staged a riot today,
One lost its thumb, what can I say?
Laughter echoes in this muddled space,
Chaos turns life into a funny race!

Juggling life's clutter, what a sight!
Crazy mishaps feel just right.
When chaos reigns, and gets my joke,
I find the fun in every poke.

The Symphony of Shattered Dreams

A trumpet's gone, a drum's not here,
They lost their way on a midnight cheer.
Pots and pans create a tune,
As I dance around my living room soon!

Notes fly off like popcorn at play,
Creating a melody of dismay.
But in this mess, oh such a thrill,
Each broken dream has its own goodwill!

Balloons float high, then meet their fate,
Bursting with laughter—what a date!
Confetti's everywhere, I've lost my shoes,
Yet in this chaos, I just can't lose!

With a mop in hand, I take a bow,
My symphony of mess, I'll show you how.
Each fallen note tells a fun little tale,
In the wreckage, my heart will sail!

Raw Beauty in the Chaos

Paint spills on a canvas of fate,
Blue meets orange—it's a colorful rate!
My hands look like an artist's dream,
Messy strokes on a wobbly theme.

Sticky fingers, a snack gone rogue,
Chocolate smears in a sugary vogue.
Who knew desserts would start a fight,
In this sweet chaos, it feels just right!

Doodles in notebooks, a wild spree,
Every line tells a secret to me.
Erased with laughter, it's all a game,
Raw beauty emerges, unashamed!

Bubbles in the bathtub, what a splash,
Rubber ducks rock while I make a crash.
In every spot that's out of place,
Lies a joy that chaos will embrace!

Chasing Whispers through Turmoil

Whispers of socks, I chase through time,
One is missing, it's a laundry crime!
Chasing down garments, what a thrill,
Hiding beneath the couch, oh what a spill!

The bathroom's a jungle, a toothpaste sea,
A toothbrush race, just wait and see.
Messes make stories, I hear them laugh,
In this whirlwind of chaos, I find my path!

The dog's gone rogue with a shoe in tow,
Dancing around like a chaos pro.
While slippers argue with the rug, oh dear,
I chase those whispers, that's the cheer!

Jumbled dreams hide in the drawer,
With giggles and glee, who could ask for more?
In every twist and turn I roam,
Turmoil's just a funny way to call it home!

Navigating the Storm of Uncertainty

Lost amidst the winds that blow,
My umbrella flipped — is this a show?
Raindrops dance on my confused head,
Should I turn back or forge ahead?

Kites are tangled in flying trees,
With squirrels giggling, feeling the breeze.
A signpost pointing — or so it seems,
To nowhere but wild, messy dreams.

Mosaic of the Wild Heart

Shards of laughter scattered wide,
In the chaos, I sometimes hide.
Colors clash like jumbled pies,
More fun than neat, oh what a surprise!

Birds with shoes and hats galore,
Strut around, what are they for?
Chasing rainbows, losing track,
In this mess, what's the hack?

Treasure Maps in Twisted Paths

X marks the spot beneath the mess,
But where's the map? I could guess!
Sticky notes on the fridge collide,
With dream notes tossed, who takes the ride?

A pirate's tale in my sock drawer,
Where treasures hide and socks just bore.
Each twist and turn a lessons blend,
Oh, what rad journeys never end.

Echoes from the Wreckage

I tripped on laughter, fell on plight,
While juggling dreams in the twilight.
Crates of chaos, stacked so high,
Echoes of hope; yeah, let's not cry!

Banana peels and pathways crossed,
In this tumble, I'm never lost.
Rebuilding joy from the uproar,
With clumsy grace, forevermore!

Through the Fractured Lens

Through shattered glass, I spy a grin,
A laugh escapes from things within.
The socks mismatched, a joyful spree,
Life's mess, a dance, just wait and see.

With crumbs on shirts and hair askew,
Chaos wears a sparkly shoe.
In each lost key, a quirky tale,
Adventures found beyond the pale.

A pickle jar turned into art,
Who knew that jams could play a part?
Glitter stuck to every chair,
A masterpiece made from thin air.

So here's to life's peculiar twists,
In playful moments, we exist.
Embrace the whirl, the laugh, the fumble,
In this grand mess, we all do tumble.

Finding Gold in the Grit

In muddy boots, we wade through strife,
Each splatter tells of prodding life.
The cake that flopped, the pie that burned,
Oh, how those lessons have been earned!

With every spill, a story brews,
Those sunscreen smudges, not just hues.
A bloom from weeds that won't give in,
Messy victories, let's begin!

Socks on the roof, a kite in flight,
Laughter echoing in the night.
From tangled cords to jumbled words,
We dance like clumsy, crazy birds.

So treasure chaos, hold it tight,
In all the blunders, there's delight.
For in the grit, we learn to shine,
A raucous blend, so divine!

Navigating the Twisted Path

With compass lost, I stroll the lane,
Avoiding puddles, dodging rain.
A squirrel scoffs, it knows the game,
Watch out for bliss—a clever claim!

In knots of string, I spot a muse,
Old coffee stains, artistic views.
A recipe gone awry, you see,
Brings forth the joy of calamity!

Down winding roads where shadows play,
I chase the sun, it leads the way.
Lost again, I find a laugh,
In every twist, a sly autograph.

Collect the stumbles, wear them proud,
Sing loud and clear amidst the crowd.
For every detour, every scrape,
Gives life a brand new shape!

Navigating the Storm's Eye

Rain-soaked shoes, a wild delight,
Dancing puddles, oh, what a sight!
With thunder's voice, I giggle and sway,
The lightning winks as if to play.

Umbrellas flipped, a comic view,
In tempest's grip, we find our crew.
A whirlwind capsizes the plainest day,
Keep spinning 'round, come what may!

The laundry flies with every gust,
In chaos, we all find a trust.
With messy hair and frizzy flair,
We toast to storms with laughs to share!

Embrace the swirl, don't hide away,
In every drizzle, let laughter stay.
For through the storm, the sunshine beams,
In crazy chaos live our dreams!

Messy Masterpieces

In a chaotic room, I trip and fall,
Paint splatters dance upon the wall.
My cat judges me with a glaring stare,
As I create art—wings in the air.

Yesterday's dinner's now today's muse,
Pasta shapes twist, oh what a ruse!
Brushes made from old spaghetti strands,
Crafting wonders from these clumsy hands.

Glue and glitter, mismatched bliss,
Each mishap sealed with a silly kiss.
The world's a canvas, wild and bright,
My mess is genius, a splendid sight.

So here I stand, a proud mess maker,
With laughter spilling, I'm no faker.
Art is perfect, or so they say,
In the mess of life, we laugh our way.

Finding the Unseen Threads

Lost my keys in the laundry bin,
Thread counts rising, oh where've they been?
Socks and grinches fist-fight at dawn,
Amid this chaos, new laughs are born.

Dinner's a riddle, I serve up a dream,
A touch of ketchup may reign supreme.
Recipes vague as my rainy day plans,
But flavors collide, sealed with my hands.

Dust bunnies dance like they own the floor,
I sweep them away, but they come back for more.
Tell me, oh fate, can mess really shine?
In this carnival of chaos—it's all divine.

A mismatched puzzle, quirky and bright,
With bloopers and blunders making it right.
Who knew life's threads were tangled and neat?
In the web of my mess, I find my seat!

Sailing Through the Silt

I've set my ship through the sea of grime,
Navigating chaos, all feels like a crime.
With jellyfish drifting, the waves laugh out loud,
As I sail through confusions, feeling quite proud.

My compass is broken, but who needs a guide?
When every wave's a rollercoaster ride.
I'll toast to the spills with a glass full of glee,
For the silt on this journey is pure jubilee.

A mermaid appears, with a brush in hand,
She paints my mishaps with a charming strand.
The ocean's a mess, yet celebrates a tune,
And I dance with the fishes beneath the bright moon.

So here's to the journey, with splashes and fun,
To messes and laughter—we've only begun.
With sails made of socks and mops for my oar,
I'm sailing through silliness, forever explore!

Symphony of the Disordered

In the kitchen chaos, pots turn to clay,
I'm mixing up magic in a quirky way.
Each utensil sings like it's lost in a dream,
Clattering harmonies, oh what a theme!

With flour storms brewing and sugar delights,
A cookie debacle takes flight on the nights.
My apron's a canvas for unfiltered jests,
Where laughter and chaos are welcomed guests.

In the clutter of life, I play all my notes,
Chasing the laughter and dodging the quotes.
For every mishap—a sonnet will bloom,
Transforming disasters into vibrant rooms.

So here's to the symphony, wild and profound,
Where disordered notes dance all around.
In each messy moment, a jubilant cheer,
With joy in the chaos, we find our frontier!

A Tapestry of Fractured Dreams

In the chaos, socks dance in pairs,
While the cat's on a mission, with no cares.
Mismatched patterns tell tales, oh so loud,
A quilt of confusion, we wear it proud.

Caffeine spills like wild confetti,
Life's a circus, and oh, so petty.
We juggle our worries, a comical show,
With laughter that bursts like popcorn aglow.

Lost keys hide in places so absurd,
Like they're on vacation, it's truly unheard.
Yet in this riddle, we find what's real,
A treasure of laughter, a whimsical deal.

So raise your glass to the mess we make,
In puddles of joy, we sip and partake.
For in tangled threads and boisterous schemes,
We weave our lives with the quirkiest dreams.

Harvesting Resilience

In gardens of chaos, weeds take their stand,
Yet there's laughter sprouting, oh isn't it grand?
We tickle the daisies, while hiccuping glee,
And plant seeds of hope with our clumsy spree.

The vegetables giggle, bizarrely misplaced,
Potatoes with hats, life's wildest embrace.
We plant our failures, watch them grow tall,
As we harvest our triumphs, we're having a ball.

We dance in the mud, with boots made of foam,
In this uproarious garden, we feel right at home.
Each stumble's a step, with a snicker or grin,
As we gather our stories, where laughter begins.

So let's toast to the mess, both silly and sweet,
For resilience blooms where the laughter's complete.
With every odd turn, we nurture delight,
In the fields of our follies, we take flight.

Cacophony of Colors

Colors collide in a raucous ballet,
With splashes of humor that brighten the gray.
The crayons are singing a topsy-turvy tune,
While paintbrushes giggle beneath a bright moon.

Splatters and drips form a wacky parade,
Where seriousness hides, all in masquerade.
Purple polka dots on a green-striped chair,
In this joyful mayhem, we float without care.

Our mishaps are canvases of cheerfully bold,
Marking the moments, both tender and cold.
We dance in the pigments, our hearts on display,
Crafting a mosaic from disarray.

So let's celebrate each crazy swirl,
Life's a wild painting – give it a twirl!
In the cacophony, we find a sweet grace,
Where laughter and color weave a warm embrace.

Stitches of Serenity

In a world of threads, we patch things just right,
With stitches of joy, and a wink of delight.
We sew up our worries, so tangled and bold,
Creating a fabric of stories retold.

Needles and laughter, they dance with each turn,
As fabric scraps whisper, 'There's wisdom to earn!'
The patterns remind us of journey and play,
Whether knotted or loose, we'll find our way.

Each flaw is a feature; each ravel, a song,
In this patchwork of life, we find we belong.
With threads of resilience, we layer our days,
In stitches of humor, our hearts hum and blaze.

So let's thread happiness through fabric divine,
In this quilt of existence, we joyfully shine.
For in every misstep, a masterpiece grows,
Crafting our lives with the laughter that flows.

Beauty in the Brokenness

Life's like a pie, with slices askew,
Whipped cream on top, but no spoon in view.
Moments all tangled, like a cat on a yarn,
We laugh at the chaos, it's our little charm.

Stumbling in rhythm, we dance on the floor,
Tripping on shoes that were left by the door.
Spilling our drinks as we giggle and cheer,
Embracing the madness, our hearts full of beer.

In the wreckage of dreams, there's treasure to seek,
A joke in the rubble, a giggle, a sneak.
Each crack tells a story, a tale of delight,
We build up our castles from remnants of fright.

So raise up a toast to the beautifully flawed,
To moments of laughter, of clumsy applaud.
In mishaps and mayhem, we find our true worth,
The beauty of life is its infinite mirth.

Sifting Through the Ashes

In the ashes of past, a spark starts to glow,
Like socks missing partners, a curious show.
We sift through the chaos, like kids in a pile,
Unearthing the giggles that make it worthwhile.

Burnt toast for breakfast, it crumbles away,
A chef's hat that's crooked, what else can we say?
Eggs dance in the pan like they've lost their routine,
We chuckle while sipping our coffee, caffeine!

Charred bits of the past hold secrets so bright,
Like marshmallows roasted in campfire's light.
We pick through the cinders, reclaiming the fun,
In each tasty failure, new laughter's begun.

So here's to our journeys, with all of their flaws,
We'll wear them like badges and give them applause.
In smudges and stains, there's a wonderland wait,
With humor our guide, we'll savor our fate.

Echoes of Order

In a world upside down, where socks are all strayed,
We giggle at dryers that have always betrayed.
With chaos a friend, we embrace the surprise,
Order's a puzzle with whimsical ties.

The dishes that tower like skyscrapers high,
A plate on a table, its balance awry.
Cocktails mixed wrong, but we raise them with cheer,
For laughter is louder when chaos is near.

Whispers of reason get lost in the fun,
Like raccoons on a mission to steal the last bun.
We waltz in the rubble, like dancers in trance,
In echoes of disorder, we find our own chance.

So here's to the madness, the quirks that we share,
To moments of laughter, our joyful affair.
With giggles and grins, let's revel and rhyme,
In echoes of order, we dance through the grime.

Lost and Found in the Disorder

In the mess of the room, where the crumbs like to play,
We search for that missing sock, it ran away.
With laughter like bubbles that float in the air,
We shrug at the clutter, it's scattered with flair.

The cat on the counter, the dog in the chair,
They judge our arrangement, must think it's a fair.
Yet amidst all the chaos, a treasure we find,
A note from the past, a spark in the mind.

So here in the whirlwind, we twirl and we spin,
With jokes that keep coming, as thick as the din.
Each moment a gem in the jumbled parade,
We laugh through the chaos; our memories made.

With smiles on our faces, we'll tackle the day,
For lost things can lead to the most silly play.
In chaos and clutter, we learn to unwind,
The joy in the disorder, a gift we can find.

Discovery in the Dirt

In the backyard, I seek my shoe,
A garden gnome waves, who knew?
Shovels and toys in a wild embrace,
Nature's mess has its own grace.

Underneath the leaves, what do I find?
A half-eaten sandwich, one of a kind!
A taco shell filled with ants on a quest,
Why clean up? This is truly the best!

Dig deeper, there's treasure in muck,
A forgotten ball and a muddy old truck.
An ecosystem thrives in my little yard,
Who needs a museum? This isn't so hard!

I plant my dreams in the chaos around,
With laughter and dirt, I dig deeper underground.
Life's adventurous, a silly delight,
In finding the lost, I feel so contrite!

Unruly Beauties

In my jungle yard, the weeds grow tall,
Meet my wildflowers, beauties after all.
Sunflowers lean like they're in a dance,
Their neighbor a dandelion, taking a chance.

The roses are laughing, with thorns in tow,
A misfit crew, putting on quite a show.
Nature's a party, uncorked and free,
Who cares about rules? Just let it be!

A rabbit hops past, wearing my shoe,
Thinks it's a hat? Well, who knew?
A squirrel glares with its nutty brigade,
In this unruly world, can't be afraid!

Snap a sweet pic; it's a riot of colors,
The beauty in chaos is for all the others.
With laughter and dirt wrapped up in delight,
Let's celebrate chaos, it feels so right!

The Treasure Beneath the Tangles

Beneath the branches and twigs that entwine,
Lies a lost golf ball, oh, how divine!
A treasure chest filled with mismatched socks,
All waiting for yarn, to gossip like clocks!

The cat's made a nest, oh what a sight,
Stuffed with fluff, just feels so right.
Leaves pose for selfies, squirrels strike a pose,
In this tangled mess, the laughter just grows.

I trip on a plant, wearing dirt as a crown,
That's just my style, in this jungle I drown.
What mysteries lie in this fussy old mess?
Each twist and each turn, brings joy, I confess.

So here's to the chaos, a grand old parade,
Life's messy adventures, in sunshine and shade.
With whispers from branches, oh what a thrill,
In tangled existence, we've found our fill!

Eclipsed by the Ordinary

In a world of chaos, the ordinary reigns,
Stuck in a sock rotate, I'm losing my gains.
A box of lost buttons, they're plotting a play,
In mismatched costumes, they dance every day.

The laundry, a mountain, spills over the bed,
Dared to climb it, now I'm filled with dread!
Underneath it all, an old remote is found,
Lost in the mess, where laughter abounds.

The plants stage a coup in the corner of gloom,
Claiming my dust bunnies as heirlooms of doom.
They plot and they scheme, oh what a team,
Their foliage dances, like they're living a dream.

Lemonade spills, and giggles are loud,
Who needs perfection when chaos is proud?
In the eclipsed moments, we truly find sun,
In the ordinary mess, life's never done!

Searching for Stars in the Gloom

In a world where socks go to hide,
Chasing dust bunnies, I'll never abide.
With each tangled scoop of note and shoe,
I laugh at the chaos trying to accrue.

Jelly spilled on the floor like art,
Echoes of laughter fill the heart.
Coffee stains my best-laid plans,
Yet somehow it all makes sense in my hands.

Dishes piled like a tower of dreams,
Each one a memory, or so it seems.
I search for constellations in the mess,
Finding joy in my daily chaos, I confess.

So here I stand, an artist of grime,
Painting my life in the rhythm of time.
In every blunder, a chance to play,
Gloom turns to giggles in a quirky ballet.

Scribbles of Serenity

On crumpled pages, my thoughts collide,
Caffeinated dreams, wide-open slide.
With doodles of dragons and cats in hats,
I find peace in the scribbles, where nonsense chats.

An ink-stained thumb's my badge of grace,
Every smudge an embrace in this chaotic space.
Like a puzzle with missing pieces galore,
I smile at the mess and look for more.

Thoughts tumble down like grapevines swing,
Each twist is a laugh: not a serious thing.
In this scribbled jumble, I'm never alone,
Finding solace in chaos that feels like home.

So grab your pencil and join the spree,
Let ink be your compass, wild and free.
Embrace the clutter, celebrate the spree,
In the scribbles of life, just let it be.

Resilience in the Fractured Light

Light bulbs flicker, my toaster explodes,
Yet here I stand, in my mismatched codes.
Chasing crumbs like they're golden stardust,
With a wink at adversity, it's a must.

Ticking clocks wear mismatched socks,
Jokes on me, while the laundry mocks.
I toast my bread with a hopeful cheer,
Knowing that laughter is always near.

In the whirl of chaos, I twirl and twist,
The drama of life, I can't resist.
A spilled drink turns into a silly dance,
In fractured light, I take a chance.

So raise a cheer for the quirks we see,
For in the mayhem, I'm truly free.
With every crack, a glittering spark,
Resilience shines bright in the shadowed park.

Unraveled but Unearthed

My plans are a tangle, a noodle soup,
Juggling dreams in a goofy loop.
Each thread I pull shows a crooked side,
Yet here in the mess, creativity's my guide.

Coffee spills and napkins fly,
I'll write a haiku, give it a try.
For every misstep on this wild spree,
I'll weld together humor and glee.

Tangled headphones and a rogue shoe lace,
In this beautiful chaos, I find my place.
Like a cat in the cupboard, I curl up tight,
Unraveled yet free in the dim twilight.

So cheers to the bundle of life's great mess,
In every blunder, there's joy to caress.
Let's toast to confusion, let laughter arise,
In this unraveled tapestry, we're all wise.

Threads of Truth

In chaos, I lost my shoe,
But found a sock that's bright sky blue.
A noodle danced upon my plate,
Declaring lunchtime is first-rate!

The cat is tangled in my hair,
With one that's stuck, it seems not rare.
A squashed tomato on my face,
Reminds me life's a funny race!

I dropped the cake; it hit the floor,
The sugar ants came in to score.
A giggle slipped, my joy renewed,
In kitchens where disaster's brewed!

Yet here I laugh and shake my head,
For in the mess, I'm well fed.
With tales to tell and smiles to share,
Who knew chaos could be so rare?

Chronicles of the Unraveled

My sweater's snagged on a door handle,
Like a ship lost, but here I dandle.
A coffee spill, a story grand,
I may be late, but life's unplanned!

The dog is chewing on my shoe,
A fashion trend that's tried and true.
With crumbs and chaos all around,
Who knew a mess could be so sound?

My plans are scribbles on a page,
Life's a stage, a humorous rage.
Like laundry left in rain to dry,
My wits have flown, I can't deny!

Yet every twist, each silly twist,
Crafts little moments not to miss.
For misadventure leads the way,
In this wild mess, I love to play!

Sunshine After the Storm

The umbrella flipped, a sail in breeze,
While puddles dare me down on knees.
A squirrel splashed with jokes in stride,
Who knew a storm could be this wide?

My hair's a frizz; oh, what a sight,
While rainbows dance with sheer delight.
I stomp on puddles, splash and cheer,
The world's a stage, I'm the premier!

These sneakers soaked, I walk on air,
Though wet, my spirits have no care.
With laughter mixed in stormy weather,
It's really fun when we're all together!

And when the clouds begin to part,
I find the joy tucked in my heart.
So splash along, let troubles flee,
For sunshine waits right here for me!

The Quiet After the Quake

After the quake, I lost my keys,
They did a dance, oh, what a tease!
A picture frame is upside down,
While my cat wears a frowning crown.

The coffee pot is now a mess,
But in its chaos, I find success.
A wiggle worm beneath my chair,
Turns frowns to giggles in the air!

I trip on toys, they own the floor,
The dust bunnies hold a lively score.
Yet in the stillness, smiles arise,
A wiggly joy, a sweet surprise!

So let the world quake, spin, and swirl,
I'll grab my hat and give a twirl.
In jumbled moments, laughter's key,
To make this mess feel fun and free!

Dancing in the Disarray

Amidst the chaos, I twirl with glee,
My socks mismatched, oh what a spree!
Spilled coffee shapes a modern art,
Who needs a plan? Let's break apart!

The floor is lava, watch me hop,
Dodging dirty laundry, I just can't stop!
Life's a jumble, toss in some flair,
Funky moves, throw caution to air!

Waltzing through stacks of unfiled bills,
Stumbling through joy with giggles and spills,
One shoe on the wrong foot, invite the fall,
In this delightful mess, I'll dance through it all!

Cheers to the clowns, let laughter abound,
In this whirlwind, our joy's the sound!
Grab a partner, let chaos take lead,
Together we'll laugh, it's all that we need!

Seeds of Hope in Dissonance

Pots and pans thrown in a bouncy ballet,
Who knew cooking could go this way?
Flour flies high like a cotton candy cloud,
In this delightful mess, I laugh out loud!

Mixing mismatched socks with my bright spatula,
Cooking's become an awkward ritual,
Dish soap bubbles do the tango, oh dear,
In this kitchen chaos, I find no fear!

Veggies wearing sunglasses, so out of style,
Tomatoes gossip, making me smile,
Each ingredient's singing its own silly song,
In disarray's charm, I feel I belong!

With a whisk in hand, mischief takes flight,
In the kitchen chaos, everything's bright,
Growing seeds of laughter, as we stir and tumble,
In dissonant joy, we proudly stumble!

Crafting Sense from Nonsense

Glue sticks and glitter cover my desk,
Crafting my heart into a fun grotesque,
Tangled strings dance with no proper design,
In knots of nonsense, my soul starts to shine!

Paper plates rocket, a spaceship in flight,
The cat's the captain, don't you think it's right?
Colors collide in a crayon fight,
In this absurdity, everything feels light!

Mismatched buttons tell stories untold,
Watch how the chaos begins to unfold,
A masterpiece born from the odd and the strange,
In silly creations, I find my exchange!

Crafting and laughing, oh what a spree!
In this joyful mess, I'm perfectly free,
Handmade glories, embraced with a grin,
Out of the nonsense, let the fun begin!

Where Wildflowers Bloom

In a garden where weeds like to play,
Wildflowers poke through in a colorful way,
Sunshine and shadows dance on each petal,
In the crooked paths, we find the metal!

A patch of daisies sings with surprise,
Sunburned squirrels share cheeky high fives,
Butterflies flutter with no hint of dread,
Amidst the clutter, whimsy is bred!

Tangled vines hold secrets and dreams,
Nature's giggles burst at the seams,
Every twist tells a tale through the grass,
In this ripped-up lane, let the laughter amass!

So here's to the mess and all the fun,
Where wildflowers bloom under the sun,
In joyful chaos, I lift up my broom,
And sweep away worries, let laughter consume!

Artisans of the Anomaly

In chaos we dance, a slapstick parade,
With mismatched socks, our plans seem to fade.
Yet laughter erupts from spills on the floor,
Crafting delight we didn't plan for.

A pickle jar opens, it bursts with delight,
While glue sticks our hopes, by default, to flight.
Juggling our dreams with a banana peel,
We twist through the mess, oh, how we feel!

The recipe calls for a dash of the famished,
Transforming the bland into something outlandish.
Artisans thrive in this wacky old tale,
With hiccups that turn into humor's great sail.

So here's to the tumbles, the fumbles, and falls,
With each little blunder, the laughter just calls.
In this wild bazaar of unplanned delight,
We're crafting our joy in the midst of the fight.

Reviving the Wreckage

From wreckage we rise, like a bird on a tire,
In each tangled mess lies absurdity's fire.
A sofa with holes is a throne for our cat,
It giggles and purrs, how silly is that?

The dishes may tower, a leaning high-rise,
But who needs a kitchen when laughter is wise?
Each splatter of sauce on the wall tells a tale,
Of feasts gone awry, yet we somehow prevail.

Jigsawed in chaos, we find hidden gems,
Like missing socks found in forgotten old hems.
We welcome the mishaps, trembling yet bold,
In our fragmented tales, laughter unfolds.

So raise up your glass, to the mess and the fun,
We're reviving the wreckage, together as one.
In every disaster, let's toast to the cheer,
For life isn't perfect, but that's part of the cheer!

Emergent Patterns

In crooked old lines, we sketch out our fate,
With crayons and giggles, we turn up the rate.
A canvas of chaos adorned with our dreams,
Emerging from laughter, with joy as our theme.

Sprinkles of chuckles on pancakes so tall,
Our breakfast gymnastics may lead to a fall.
The syrup we spill tells a story unique,
Of mornings that burst with a whimsical squeak.

We tumble through puzzles, a jigsaw of fun,
With pieces misplaced, but we're still on the run.
What's perfect, we ask, in this jumble of light?
Patterns emerge in the mess, oh, what a sight!

So dance through the slip-ups, rejoice with the glee,
In the mayhem we find our own jubilee.
With sketches of life that aren't drawn quite so neat,
We celebrate patterns that make us complete.

Ode to the Misfit Moments

Here's to the squabbles and quirky mistakes,
When life tosses curveballs, we giggle and quake.
A cake that collapses, a party unplanned,
In misfit moments, we all take a stand.

The socks in a tumble, like dancers in pairs,
Declare that perfection just isn't our care.
With each silly mishap that enters our realm,
We ride on the waves, let silliness helm.

Forgotten appointments that turn into fate,
We trip on our words, then we celebrate.
In the quirks and the flops, there's a treasure to find,
An ode to the moments we've unconfined.

So raise up your glass, to the blunders we cheer,
For each misfit moment brings laughter near.
In the tapestry woven with joy and a grin,
We honor the chaos, the mess we're all in.

The Art of Unraveling

In tangled yarns of daily life,
We trip on laughter, dance with strife.
A sock that's lost, a pen that bleeds,
Each blunder sowing silly seeds.

With coffee spills and missing keys,
We find ourselves on bended knees.
Yet in the chaos, we can see,
A joy that comes from simply free.

Like cats that leap and land askew,
We learn to laugh at our own view.
Embrace the mess, the clumsy fun,
In every stumble, we have won.

So grab your kite, let wild winds blow,
We'll weave our dreams in row by row.
For in the wild, untamed distress,
We craft our lives and learn to dress.

Reclaiming the Shattered Pieces

A plate once whole becomes confetti,
Mom said it's fine, the heart's still ready.
We gather shards of memories bright,
And grin at how they catch the light.

With every crack, a story's told,
Of midnight snacks and dreams of gold.
We piece together laughter's cheer,
And toast each mess with hearty beer.

In puddles formed from coffee fights,
We splash around with pure delight.
Each break a chance to start anew,
Life's quirks reflecting shades of blue.

So here's to glue and joyful art,
Transforming woes into a chart.
For in the rubble, joy finds grace,
A dance of mishaps in our space.

Glimpses of Grace

In squeaky shoes that trip and slide,
We waltz through life, we bump, we glide.
A wayward cat, a misplaced sock,
Each misfit puzzle binds the block.

With coffee stains on canvas bright,
We laugh at chaos, pure delight.
An unexpected spin of fate,
Unraveling humor, isn't it great?

We twirl through moments, a merry-go,
Finding joy in what's often slow.
Every mishap is a painted hue,
A glimpse of grace in all we do.

So raise a glass of clumsy cheer,
To spilled secrets and our dear.
For in the mess, we clearly see,
Life's perfect dance of you and me.

Sculpting Light from Shadows

Through tangled vines and curious bends,
We sculpt the light that laughter lends.
A wayward shoe, a splattered slide,
We paint our joy with messed-up pride.

In every tumble, a chance to play,
We craft our path in a quirky way.
With giggles echoing in the dark,
We find delight, we find our spark.

From scattered crumbs to cheerful spills,
Each wobbly moment surely thrills.
In shadows cast by silly plight,
We dance through mishaps, holding tight.

So let the chaos reign and grow,
In woven tales, our laughter flows.
For in the blur, the joy doth show,
We sculpt our lives from ebb and flow.

Serendipity Amongst the Struggle

When laundry's piled and dishes stack,
I trip on toys, and that's a fact.
But in the mess, I start to see,
A treasure map that's drawn for me.

A lost sock hides beneath the chair,
With crumbs that whisper, 'Don't despair!'
For laughter fills the cluttered room,
And giggles grow among the gloom.

I dance with dust bunnies in sight,
Turning chaos into delight.
So, while the world's a bit askew,
I wear a crown that's made for two.

From tangled cords a song will rise,
Our family jam, a sweet surprise.
Turn up the volume, let's embrace,
The joyful noise that fills this space.

Navigating the Maze

I wandered deep through my own hall,
With snack wrappers stuck to the wall.
The floor's a puzzle, truth be told,
Yet every step is brave and bold.

Behind the couch, a lost treasure lies,
An ancient coin, or maybe fries?
Each twist and turn, a laugh or two,
In this quirky maze, I find my crew.

I map the crumpled pizza box,
With a pen that's shaped just like a fox.
Who needs a plan, it's all a game,
In this chaotic life, it's never lame.

So here's to us, the brave, the bold,
Who navigate the mess like gold.
We're champions of the messy space,
With smiles that light up every trace.

Treasures in the Turmoil

Among the clutter, there's a charm,
A rubber duck, it keeps me warm.
I forge a path through scattered toys,
In the chaos, I find my joys.

Spilled cereal becomes confetti bright,
As we dance around this mess tonight.
Unmatched socks are now a game,
Each one's a fighter, never the same.

From sticky hands to laughter loud,
We make our way through the chaotic crowd.
In every spill, a splash of cheer,
I find my heart, I hold it near.

In tangled cords, creativity flows,
A masterpiece where anything goes.
With open arms, embrace the wild,
In every mess, we remain a child.

Cracks that Let the Light In

In a world that spills and breaks apart,
I collect the shards, a work of art.
From all the cracks, a story weaves,
Through every hurdle, laughter leaves.

With mismatched shoes and hair amiss,
I twirl in chaos, can't resist.
The juggling act of life so grand,
Together we rise, hand in hand.

A coffee stain turns into a smile,
And time slows down, let's stay awhile.
With goofy grins, we take a chance,
In every blunder, we find our dance.

So raise a toast to mess and mud,
To all the joys that come from crud.
For through the cracks, the light peeks in,
In sweetest chaos, we begin.

The Dance of Disorder

In socks mismatched, I twirl around,
With cereal stuck to the kitchen ground.
A dance of chaos, a step or two,
Who knew this mess could feel so new?

Bananas on the shelf in dismay,
While laundry waits for a sunny day.
The cat strikes a pose in a pile of clothes,
Oh, what a life, without any prose!

Dishes stacked, a tower of dreams,
Lost in the swirl of wiggly streams.
My coffee's cold, but I'm warm inside,
In this jumbled joy, I take my stride.

So here's to clutter, here's to the spree,
Where laughter lives and chaos is free.
With every stumble and every fall,
I find my rhythm, embracing it all.

Messages in the Madness

A toaster that talks, or maybe I'm wrong,
Whispers of crumbs make the morning long.
A jigsaw of thoughts with pieces astray,
In this puzzling life, I laugh all day.

Leftovers dance in a tupperware sight,
While socks plot revolts in the middle of night.
Frying pan symphonies, tune in the air,
Who needs perfect when chaos is fair?

A shoe with a sock, a hat out of place,
The dog takes a leap in a wild little race.
A message in madness, it's clear as day,
That laughter can bloom where messes at play.

So grab your whimsy, let worries float by,
In the whirl of the wacky, just give it a try.
In this tangled adventure, oh what a sight,
We find joy in the chaos, dancing at night.

Elegant Entropy

Oh, look at the table, it's a work of art,
With coffee cups stacked like a whimsical chart.
My plants are conspiring, they seem to agree,
That tangled, dear chaos is how it should be.

A crayon drawing my kid made last spring,
Is stuck on the fridge with a magnety zing.
In errant pencils and papers that fly,
I discover a world where laughs pile high.

The world spins wild, a topsy-turvy play,
Yet in every odd corner, I find my way.
The fridge hums a tune, the clock's off the beat,
In this elegant mess, life feels so sweet!

So let's raise a toast with a glass half empty,
To moments of joy, with plenty of sentry.
In this chaos of colors, let's twirl and embrace,
The beauty in blunders, in this lively space.

The Light Within the Fray

In the kitchen, a constant debate,
Is it a pan or a stage—who can relate?
Spaghetti jungle, a sauce avalanche,
Dinner could win in a chaotic dance!

Colorful crumbs scatter across the blue rug,
While socks hold a secret with every snug hug.
Chaos unfolds, like a comedic show,
In this hilarious life, I steal the flow.

Oranges tumble, roll back to their aim,
Finding purpose, oh what a game!
Suddenly, I trip on a toy on the floor,
Yet laughter erupts, I can't help but roar.

So here's to the madness, let's cherish the rush,
With every wild moment, we revel and crush.
The light within fray, it shines ever so bright,
In this whirlwind of life, we dance through the night.

Blossoms Amongst the Rubble

In the chaos of my sock drawer,
A lone sock winks, a smile to score.
Dust bunnies dance, they take a stance,
Who knew laundry brought such romance?

Between the crumbs of yesterday's snack,
A toaster hums, there's no lack.
Spilled coffee cups, my morning muse,
They paint a story I can't refuse.

Oh, mismatched spoons sing harmony,
Confetti from a birthday spree!
In clutter's embrace, I find my bliss,
A treasure map I couldn't miss.

So here's to life's delightful mess,
In every chaos, we find success.
Amongst the rubble, blooms a jest,
In laughter's arms, we are so blessed.

Chaos as Canvas

My kitchen is a modern art,
With splatters that make the chefs depart.
Egg shells hop like little spry,
A masterpiece that'll make you cry.

Pasta's painted on the wall,
My recipe's a free-for-all.
Flour clouds like a winter storm,
In this wild art, I find my form.

Chopsticks fly like they know the way,
One missed catch at the end of the day.
But laughter lingers in the air,
As toast pops up, without a care.

In the mayhem, I find my groove,
A dance with chaos, oh, how it soothes!
With each mishap, my heart expands,
Creating joy with messy hands.

Radiance in Unruly Moments

In the tangled hair of my dog's tail,
Lies a story that's destined to sail.
With furballs flying, they do their dance,
Who knew mischief could lead to romance?

A cat on the counter with a cheeky grin,
Knocking down whatever's within.
Adventures happen when pets run free,
They teach us how fun spills can be.

In the cluttered mess of toys amassed,
Laughter rings out, shadows are cast.
We create a kingdom, both wild and bright,
In every disaster, there's pure delight.

Oh, the giggles that rise with each tumble,
Chasing chaos, we never grumble.
For in these moments, crazy and wide,
We find that love and joy abide.

The Alchemy of Ruin

Muffin crumbs are magic dust,
Transforming floors, it's a must.
Spilled soda, a fizzy art,
Crafting joy, a quirky part.

My closet's a pandemonium show,
Old shirts speaking in whispers low.
A treasure trove of forgotten dreams,
Among the wreckage, sunlight beams.

In mismatched socks, adventure blooms,
As mismatched plates fill cozy rooms.
Even chaos can wear a crown,
Turning frowns into a golden gown.

Oh, the jests within life's disarray,
A comedy play in a messy ballet.
With each blunder, I learn to jest,
In the alchemy of ruin, we are blessed.

Reclaiming Order from the Whirlwind

In a room of mismatched socks,
Spinning like a wobbly clock,
Plates stacked high, a tower of lies,
I search for sanity with squinty eyes.

Dust bunnies dance in a conga line,
They've made a home in the corner, divine.
With every step, I trip and spin,
A ballet of chaos, where to begin?

Grocery lists turned paper cranes,
Lost in the whirlwind, but who remains?
As I juggle the clutter like a clown,
I laugh as my calmness tumbles down.

Yet amid the chaos, a goldfish grin,
A treasure lurks underneath the din.
With every stashed toy and random shoe,
I find joy peeking through the mess, too!

Harmony in the Haphazard

My coffee mug sits on a pile of junk,
Like a captain lost on a shipwrecked trunk.
To-do lists scribbled on napkins, oh dear,
Yet in this tangle, there's something clear.

Bananas beside old coins and keys,
I serenade the chaos with whimsical ease.
The couch is a landscape of cushions askew,
In this art of disorder, something feels true.

A spoon in the fridge, a sock on a plant,
Life's hilarious puzzle, quite nonchalant.
From clutter I conjure a symphony sweet,
Like a dance party's rhythms beneath my feet.

So raise your glass to the mess we adore,
A cacophony of life, with laughter galore.
Through topsy-turvy, a giggle ignites,
In the whirlwind, we find our delights!

Whispers in the Chaos

Dishes are stacked like a game of Jenga,
A wobbly tower that could use a benga.
Socks in the fridge and spoons in the loo,
In this madness, what's a girl to do?

Laughter echoes under cluttered skies,
I peek through the pile and close my eyes.
Whispers of order call out from beneath,
There's charm in the clutter, though I see teeth.

A cat on my laptop, a dog on my book,
In this creature chaos, just take a look.
As I tiptoe through papers and dust on the floor,
Every misstep within opens up door.

So raise your chin, take a breath, realize,
The beauty in jumbles and life's silly ties.
In this whirlwind dance, look around and see,
Whispers of joy in sweet disarray's spree!

Fragments of Clarity

Puzzle pieces scattered all on the ground,
In this foggy maze, who is-so profound?
Coffee stains form stories on pages of old,
A treasure map woven in moments of bold.

The laundry fights back, a colorful war,
While the dust bunnies gather in colorful score.
A shoe for a hat, and a broom as my staff,
In this ruckus of treasures, I giggle and laugh.

Old receipts linger like ghosts from the past,
With numbers and scribbles, I'm spellbound at last.
Each scrap of paper, a memory's muse,
In the realm of the messy, there's nothing to lose.

So let's raise our glasses with joyful cheer,
To the chaos that whispers so sweet in our ear.
Fragments of clarity, hidden and wild,
In the joyful disarray, forever a child!

Chaos as Canvas

In a room full of clutter, I toe on a shoe,
A bright purple sock, with a big hole, too.
Birds in my hair, free as can be,
I laugh at the chaos that dances around me.

Crayons on the floor, paper in my hair,
I sculpt a fine mess, like a piece of flair.
With pizza sauce splatters, an abstract delight,
I raise up my brush to paint through the night.

A parrot with leggings and shades on its beak,
Whispers sweet nothings, but can't even speak.
In this gallery of giggles, I dart and I sway,
Who knew such disorder could bring out my play?

So bring on the chaos, the spills and the stains,
With each little mishap, creativity reigns.
In laughter, we stumble, we trip and we slide,
Turning life's chaos into a joyride.

Lessons from the Wreckage

Under the table, a treasure I find,
Leftover snacks of the strangest kind.
Old homework crumpled, a fish toy, too,
What lessons are hiding? Well, I'll find a few!

Mismatched socks on the floor like confetti,
I wonder if they'd dance if they were ready.
A half-dried paintbrush, oh what a sight,
It once colored the world, now stuck in the light.

I open my closet, and what do I see?
A three-piece suit from an old style spree!
Who wore this attire? I can only guess,
Life's full of surprises, the kind you can't stress.

So let's cheer for the wrinkled, the shabby, the torn,
In each little wreckage, new ideas are born.
With a giggle and grin, I declare it's okay,
To stumble through life in the silliest way.

Music in the Mayhem

A symphony plays from my kitchen tonight,
With forks on the floor and the cat in mid-flight.
Whisking the chaos, we dance to the mess,
Who knew that missteps could bring such finesse?

The blender's a drummer, the fridge hums along,
While the toaster just pops to its jamming song.
I step on a squeaky toy, and what a surprise!
It's the lead rapper waking the neighbors' goodbyes!

In chaotic harmony, we twirl and we sway,
Each wobble we make is a dance of cliché.
With laughter as music, we revel in glee,
In this concert of chaos, oh how wild we be!

So gather your misfit friends, hold them tight,
We'll make music in mayhem and dance through the night.
In the rhythm of nonsense, together we'll sing,
This glorious mess, oh the joy it can bring!

Harmony in Haphazard

Life's a puzzle with mismatched pieces,
A duck in a hat and a cat that fiercely leases.
Upside-down photos, and socks on the wall,
In this haphazard haven, we giggle and crawl.

Spills on the counter, a slippery floor,
Makes every step feel like a fun dance encore.
With a sprinkle of chaos, we stir up delight,
Who knew that the jumble could set hearts alight?

In the garden, a scarecrow craves haute couture,
While broccoli dreams of being a lure.
We celebrate odd balls, let the weirdness unfold,
In this whimsical world, we'll be brave and bold.

So here's to the mess and the charming disorder,
Where laughter and joy are the tale's true recorder.
In the harmony found in this curious play,
We thrive in the haphazard, come what may!

Puzzles of the Heart

My heart's a puzzle, pieces askew,
Like socks in the dryer, I haven't a clue.
I search in the fridge, I check under the bed,
It seems I misplaced love, just like my left shoe.

I trip over feelings, I slip on my fears,
Like finding old crumbs and dodging the tears.
Each laugh feels like glue, binding mess to the fun,
I'll sort out the chaos with pizza and beers.

The clues that I gather, some wild, some absurd,
Like a cat chasing shadows, in utterly blurred.
Yet each twist and turn, is a joke and a jest,
Life's comedy show, where silliness stirred.

So here in the chaos, I twirl and I spin,
Embracing the whimsy, the loud laugh within.
For even in madness, a dance can be found,
As I puzzle together the mess that is kin.

Emergence from the Embers

From ashes I emerge, a phoenix with flair,
With marshmallows stuck, in my messy hair.
I laugh at the flames that once held me tight,
S'mores for my heart, I roast what I bear.

The smoke may get thick, like a plot full of lies,
But I wave to the sparks as they flicker and rise.
Who knew messy moments could light up the sky?
With each tasty fail, I bloom, much to my surprise.

My heart's a campfire, where stories unfold,
With a sprinkle of chaos, and some laughter bold.
Each ember can warm us, if we're willing to play,
As we dance in the warmth of the stories retold.

So here's to the flare-ups, the laughs that we share,
In the charred bits of life, I find joy everywhere.
From the mess of the flame, I rise with a grin,
Emerging from embers, my heart laid bare.

Serenity in Turmoil

A calm in the storm, I sip on my tea,
While chaos around me is wild and free.
I bob like a cork in the ocean's wild swell,
Serenity's hiding behind shelves of debris.

With laundry a mountain and dishes a sea,
I whirl through the mess, like a leaf on a spree.
Each sigh's an adventure, each giggle a shout,
In this lively tornado, there's peace, can't you see?

I dance with the chaos, I skip with delight,
Like a cat in a hat, in the midst of the night.
The whirlwind spins round, and I twirl through it all,
Finding calm in the circus, as laughter takes flight.

So dance with the ruckus, embrace the buffet,
As life serves up chaos in a colorful way.
For underneath clutter, we shine just like stars,
Serenity's waiting, in the mess of the day.

Roses from the Rubble

In a heap of old junk, I spotted a bloom,
A rose in the rubble, defying the gloom.
With petals of chaos, 'neath weeds that entwine,
It giggles at trouble, dispelling the doom.

I trip on my dreams, while I waltz through despair,
My clumsy old heart finds a rhythm to share.
Each thistle's a dancer, each thorn's got a story,
A bouquet of blunders, I proudly declare.

So here in the mess, laughter sprouts like a vine,
With flavors that tingle, and moments divine.
I'll pluck every bloom, in this garden of glee,
Crafting roses from rubble, one giggle at a time.

So let the world tumble, let it twist and turn,
In the dance of the awkward, there's much to discern.
For from every misstep, a flower can rise,
Embracing life's quirks, I've got plenty to learn.

Lost in the Tangled Thread

In the closet, sweaters collide,
Scarves entwined, like they've got pride.
I thought I'd dress with style and flair,
But I look like a scarf-wearing bear.

Socks performing an odd ballet,
Two left feet just want to play.
Who needs a match? It's quite absurd,
Solo socks, the lost and heard.

Comb through chaos, what do I seek?
A rogue button giving me a peek.
With every tug, a laugh erupts,
In tangled threads, joy corrupts.

Yet in this mess, a lesson's spun,
Life's like laundry; it's all just fun.
So I'll embrace this fashion show,
In a world where colors boldly glow.

Chaos Breeds Clarity

In a kitchen, pots engage in strife,
Baking flour arguing with a knife.
Eggshells crack, they jump and shout,
Where's the calm in this food fight bout?

A blender's whir, like a wild dance,
Chopped veggies spin, no second chance.
Yet somehow, the soup tastes divine,
Chaos on the stove, oh my, how it shines!

Lemon skins bounce from floor to wall,
While the toaster sends forth its call.
Who knew that mess could spark delight?
Cooked up giggles in the kitchen light.

So here's to chaos, that zany spree,
Cooking mishaps set our spirits free.
In every splatter, laughter's the key,
To find joy in the absurdity!

Amidst the Jumbled Journey

Maps crumpled in the glove box mess,
Directions lost, what a large test!
GPS on break, so now what's next?
Adventure waits, I'm feeling perplexed.

Wandered off to who-knows-where,
Road signs dance, I pull at my hair.
But the views are wild, oh what a prize!
Nature's canvas, a grand surprise.

Every bump leads to giggles shared,
With every wrong turn, I'm unprepared.
Yet laughter lifts, our spirits align,
In this jumbled ride, joy is the sign!

So let the compass spin like a top,
For in every detour, we'll never stop.
In a journey full of silly glee,
We're lost together, just you and me.

Resilience in the Ruins

Amidst the rubble, a cat has a nap,
Chilling in piles of old junk and scrap.
While I ponder life, oh what a sight,
A meow says, 'Chill, everything's alright!'

Broken pots tell tales of days gone by,
Grass grows wild where dreams used to fly.
Yet weeds sprout gems among the decay,
In this chaos, humor finds its way.

With every crack, a chuckle stirs,
In every flaw, a story purrs.
Why fix what's cracked, it's alright to sway,
In ruins, laughter becomes the play.

So here's to the mess where wild things grow,
Finding a smile in the afterglow.
For in the mayhem, we gleefully see,
Resilience blooms; just let it be!

Fragments of Clarity

In a room full of socks, where did they go?
The search for a partner leads to a show!
A single shoe hints at a dance not done,
While the cat claims the pillow, oh what fun!

Toothpaste on the mirror, a masterpiece bright,
The kids threw their crayons, it's a colorful sight.
Amidst the chaos, laughter rings clear,
Finding treasure in cushions, a ball from last year!

Chairs are towering, a ladder of fate,
We wear mismatched socks; is it too late?
An outlandish party in the middle of mess,
Suddenly those crumbs feel like soul food bless!

Juggling our lives with a wink and a grin,
Who needs perfection when chaos can win?
Crafting laughter from crumbs on the floor,
Embracing the silly, we always want more!

Dancing on the Edge of Disorder

A blender in reverse and a pancake flops,
As flour flies high, everyone stops.
A dance in the kitchen, syrupy delight,
Sticky hands wave, oh what a sight!

The dog's in the laundry, in socks it does roll,
Bouncing with joy, it's gained control.
A t-shirt with stains, art on display,
Wearing our mess like it's just another day!

Murky coffee spills like a Jackson Pollock,
We laugh as the clock strikes a laughter-filled frock.
The music of chaos plays loud and clear,
A symphony of giggles rings in each ear.

On the edge of nonsense, we twirl and laugh,
Disorder's our partner in this crazy_half.
With every misstep, we dance and we cheer,
Finding joy in the wild, through every veneer!

The Art of Assembling Shadows

Paperclips mingle like friends at a bar,
A sandwich half-eaten, our own bizarre star.
The couch swallows secrets, old snacks it keeps,
Conversations in shadow where clutter still creeps.

Under the bed, an army of dust bunnies rise,
Their fluffy resilience is quite the surprise.
A sock lost in battle, now a war-torn flag,
Adventurers of chaos in an old shopping bag!

The shadowy corners tell tales with a grin,
Like mischievous sprites hiding within.
An abstract assembly of laughter and glee,
We toast to the chaos, it's art, don't you see?

Stringing moments together, they form a light,
From the mess of our days, we create delight.
No frame can contain this beauty we've found,
In the gallery of life, our joy knows no bound!

Serendipity Amongst the Scraps

A rogue potato rolls under the chair,
Searching for friends in the dust-ridden air.
A puzzle with pieces that surely don't fit,
Guessing the picture we'll call it a hit!

Paper scraps scattered, a kid's craft parade,
The dog steals a sandwich, what a grand escapade!
With crayons on walls like a modern art show,
We laugh at the madness and let the joy flow.

Those mismatched plates hold a story or two,
Made from our journeys, each chip tells what's true.
The midnight snack raid, oh what a delight,
A feast of leftovers on a plate in the night!

So gather your scraps, let's make something bold,
The beauty of chaos is a treasure untold.
In the mess of the day, we twirl and we sway,
Celebrating the silly, in our quirky ballet!

www.ingramcontent.com/pod-product-compliance
Lightning Source LLC
Chambersburg PA
CBHW051654160426
43209CB00004B/899